W9-CSK-574

DINOSAURS

by Doug DuBosque

PEEL
Growing books for growing people!

Peel Productions • Vancouver WA

Learn about other books
in this series online at
drawbooks.com!

Copyright ©1993-2014 Douglas C. DuBosque. All rights reserved, including the right of reproduction in whole or in part, in any form.

Published by Peel Productions, Inc., Vancouver, Washington USA

Amazon print-on-demand edition
ISBN 0-939217-93-7
ISBN 978-0939217-93-9

Cataloging-in-Publication Data

DuBosque, D. C.
　　Draw dinosaurs / by Doug DuBosque
　　　　　p.　　cm.
　　Revision of: c1993
　　Includes index.
　　Summary: provides step-by-step instructions for drawing dinosaurs one line at a time or for beginning with ovals, triangles, and solid forms.
　　ISBN
　　1. Dinosaurs in art--Juvenile literature. 2. Drawing--technique--Juvenile literature. [1. Dinosaurs in art. 2. Drawing--Technique.] I. Title.
NC780.5.D83 1997
743.6--dc21

97-24684

DINOSAURS

Contents

Rods and Joints

Look carefully at this *Tyrannosaurus* skeleton.

Can you find the shoulder joint? The knee?

Can you see where the legs and arms bend?

To make the legs of a dinosaur look good in your drawing, look at the skeleton whenever you can. You can find many on the internet by doing an image search.

Draw *rods* (lines) to show parts of arms and legs. Draw *joints* (circles) where they connect and bend.

rod

joint

hip

From this angle, one hip joint lies directly behind the other, so you only see the closer one.

Always draw rods and joints very lightly, so you can either erase them or cover them with shading. You don't want them as part of your final drawing, but they do give you a powerful tool to use along the way!

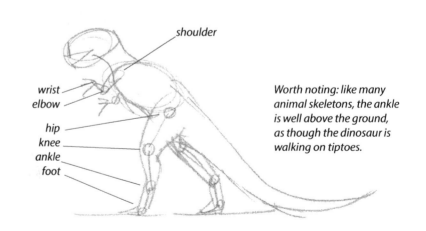

shoulder

wrist
elbow

hip
knee
ankle
foot

Worth noting: like many animal skeletons, the ankle is well above the ground, as though the dinosaur is walking on tiptoes.

Always start out *lightly!*

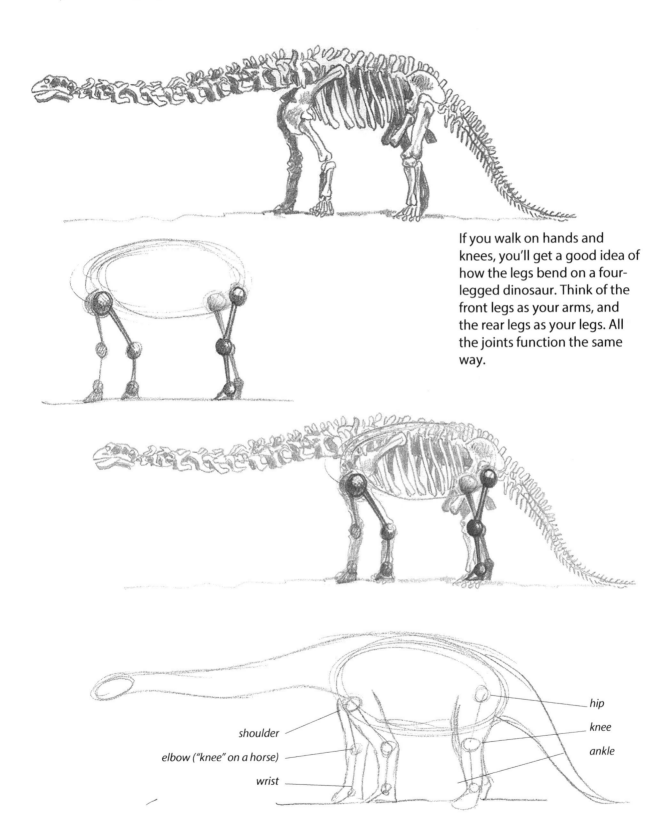

If you walk on hands and knees, you'll get a good idea of how the legs bend on a four-legged dinosaur. Think of the front legs as your arms, and the rear legs as your legs. All the joints function the same way.

shoulder

elbow ("knee" on a horse)

wrist

hip

knee

ankle

Supplies

You can draw with just about anything.

People in caves used dried clay and black stuff out of the fire pit, and we're still talking about their drawings 25,000 years later!

But caves, charcoal, mud and torches do not make for an optimal drawing environment. So start with a comfortable place to draw – with decent light, so you can see what you're doing.

- Draw with a pencil that's longer than your finger.

- Sharpen your pencil when it gets dull!

- Find an eraser – the one on your pencil will disappear quickly.

- For practice drawings, use recycled paper – for example, draw on the back of old photocopies or computer printouts.

- Plan to keep your drawings – you'll find instructions for a simple portfolio on page 62.

Positive attitude!

Persistence!

Practice!

Linosaurs

Sometimes, you can make a
dinosaur starting with simple
lines.

Can you spot the dinosaurs
lurking in these curves?

Camarasaurus

CAM-AR-A-SAW-RUS

"Chambered lizard"

Late Jurassic; Colorado, Wyoming, Utah and Oklahoma USA. Up to 60 feet (18m) long; weighed perhaps 20 tons. Because of long nasal openings on the top of its skull, some people think it had a trunk like an elephant (draw that if you want)!

Draw a long, swooping line.

Add a partial circle hanging from the middle of it.

Draw another line to complete the tail.

Add another line for the neck. Draw the mouth.

Always start out *lightly!*

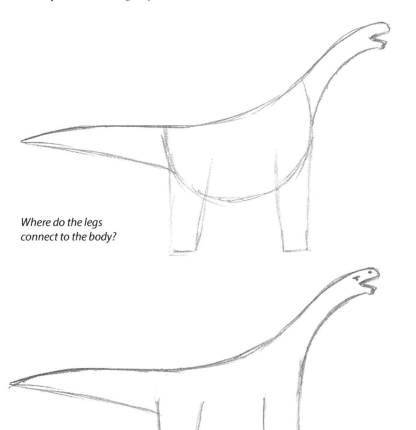

Where do the legs connect to the body?

Now draw the legs. The legs are straight in this standing dinosaur, so you don't need to draw rods and joints.

Add the eye, a nostril, and toe nails. Carefully erase lines you no longer need: in the legs, on the tail, and on the neck.

Finish your drawing by adding texture, shading, and background *(see pages 60-61 for ideas).*

While your pencil is sharp, go over fine details and clean up lines. As it gets duller, use it to add shading.

Turn your drawing as you draw to avoid smudging it with your hand.

Look at your drawing in a mirror (or from the back of the paper) to spot areas that don't look right.

Allosaurus

AL-o-SAW-rus

"Other lizard"

Late Jurassic; North America, Africa,
Australia, perhaps Asia. Up to 39 feet
(12m) long; weighed 1-2 tons. Lived long
before Tyrannosaurus, and had longer
arms with strong claws to hold its prey
while it tore at it with teeth serrated like
steak knives.

Start this drawing with a
swooping line. Draw lightly!

Draw another line above the
first, starting at one end and
ending in the middle.

From the top line, add a
smooth, curving line to
complete the tail. At the other
end, add lines for the neck and
head. Make a bump where the
eye will go. Leave room for the
mouth.

Now lightly draw the leg. You
may find it helpful to start
with rods and joints (see
pages 4-5).

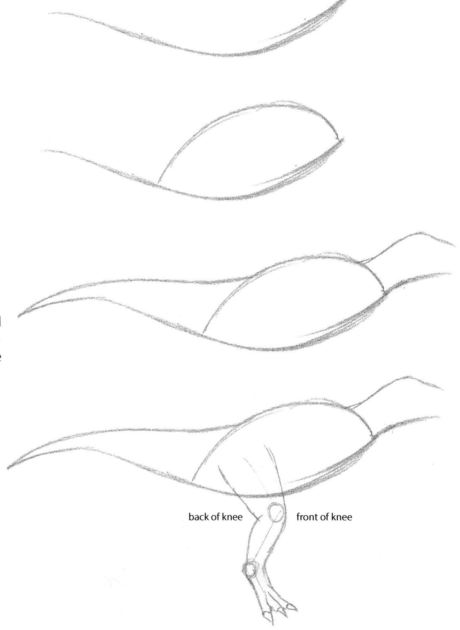

back of knee   front of knee

Add the other leg. Now your dinosaur looks as though it's moving!

Draw the arm.

Draw the other arm. Now add nose, nostril, eye, and mouth.

Finish your drawing by adding texture, shading, and background. Clean up any smudges with your eraser.

Awesome Allosaurus!

Remember to turn your drawing as you draw, so you don't accidentally smudge it with your hand.

Stenonychosaurus

STEN-OH-NIKE-O-SAW-RUS

"Narrow claw lizard"

Cretaceous; southern Alberta, Canada. 6 feet (2m) long; weighed 60-100 lbs (27-45 kg). Has been called the most intelligent dinosaur because of its large brain size (relatively speaking), which probably gave it fast reflexes for catching small prey.

Start with a long slanting and curving line. Draw another curved line under it.

Using circles for the joints, add the top part of the leg. Note how the leg overlaps the rear of the body.

Now add the thinner bottom of the leg, and the foot. Pay close attention to the details of the foot!

When you've completed the first leg, draw the second.

Always start out *lightly!*

Lightly draw another line to complete the tail. Add a line for the bottom of the neck. Lightly draw the outline of the head.

Add the eye and mouth. Draw arms, making small circles where the elbows bend. Draw the hands.

Finish your drawing by adding texture, shading, and background.

Stunning Stenonychosaurus!

While your pencil is sharp, go over fine details and make lines cleaner. As it gets duller, use it to add to the shading.

Ouranosaurus

OO-RAN-O-SAW-RUS

"Brave monitor lizard"

Early cretaceous; Niger, West Africa. Ate plants. 23 feet (7m) long. Had a tall fin along its back and tail, probably for regulating body temperature. Closely related to Iguanodon, and like it had spike-like thumbs.

Start with a long, swooping line for the back. Add a curving line underneath for the bulk of the body.

Draw two lines for the neck. Add another line to make the bottom of the tail.

Lightly draw the head. Add mouth and eye.

Look at the leg, and see how it bends in two places. Draw it, very lightly at first, starting with rods and joints (see pages 4-5).

Always start out lightly!

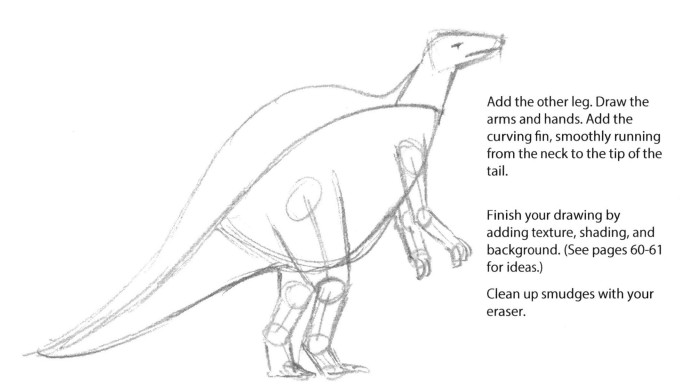

Add the other leg. Draw the arms and hands. Add the curving fin, smoothly running from the neck to the tip of the tail.

Finish your drawing by adding texture, shading, and background. (See pages 60-61 for ideas.)

Clean up smudges with your eraser.

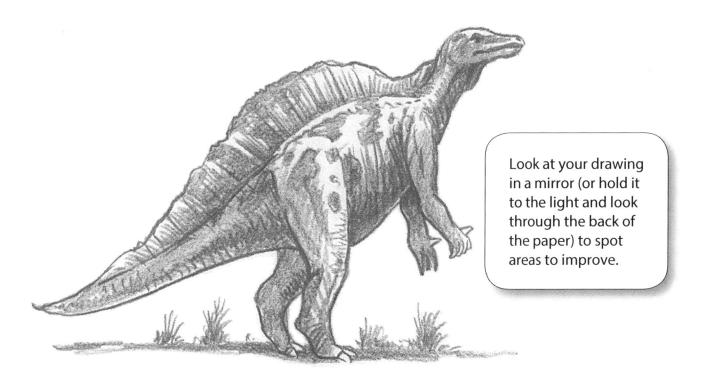

Look at your drawing in a mirror (or hold it to the light and look through the back of the paper) to spot areas to improve.

Anchiceratops

AN-KI-SER-A-TOPS

"Close-horned face"

Cretaceous; Alberta, Canada. Ate plants. 20 feet (6m) long. Had a long neck frill and one long horn above each eye, with a smaller one on the nose. The frill was probably for display, not for defense.

Start with a curved line for the back of Anchiceratops. Draw lightly at first!

Add another curving line for the bottom of the body. Look how it curves upward where the tail connects.

Notice where the front leg attaches to the body. Draw the legs, lightly at first, using rods and joints (pages 4-5).

Notice that the legs bend toward each other.

Draw the other two legs. Draw the beak-like mouth, and the armored frill that protects the dinosaur's neck. Look how far back it goes.

horns overlap

Draw a small horn on the nose, and two spiky horns behind it. Notice that they overlap. Draw the eye.

Add little horns (like toe nails) at the back of the frill protecting its neck.

Finish your drawing by adding texture, shading, and background.

Tuojiangosaurus

TWA-JAN-GO-SAW-RUS

"Tuojiang lizard"

Late Jurassic; south-central China. Ate plants, probably grazing like a horse. 20 feet (6m) long. Of all Stegosaurus-type skeletons found in Asia, this one is the best preserved.

Always start out lightly!

Draw a long line, curving up from the tail and back down to the end of the nose. Add another curve for the belly.

Draw additional lines to complete the head and tail.

Draw legs. Make the back legs bigger and longer than the front legs.

Always start out lightly!

pointy plates

spikes

Add two more legs. Draw spikes on the tail and pointy plates on the back.

Add the eye and mouth. Erase lines where tail and legs overlap the body.

To add depth to your drawing, make a second row of pointy plates.

Finish your drawing by adding texture, shading, and background.

- While your pencil is sharp, go over fine details and make lines cleaner. As it gets duller, add shading.

- Turn your drawing as you draw to avoid smudging it with your hand.

- Finally, clean up any smudges with your eraser.

Dsungaripterus

TSUN-GA-RIP-TER-US

Early Cretaceous. Skull 16 inches (41cm) long. Unusual upward-curving beak – for eating shellfish and snails? Who knows?

Dsungaripterus was a type of Pterosaur (TER-o-sor). Pterosaurs weren't actually dinosaurs, they were flying reptiles.

Start with a slanting line for the main axis of the body.

At a right angle, draw the curving lines of the head. Add the eye.

Add lines for the top of the wings, and the fingers where the wing bends.

Add curved lines for the bottom of each wing. Draw feet, and the oval at the end of the tail.

Finally, draw the lines of the arms and a few veins in the wing. Add shading.

Ovalsaurs

It's great to be able to draw a dinosaur in one position. But what if you want to draw it moving around?

How could you make it reach for food in a tree?

Or walk?

You'll gain flexibility in drawing different dinosaur poses when you start your drawing with ovals.

Apatosaurus

A-PAT-O-SAW-RUS

"Deceptive reptile"

Late Jurassic; Colorado, Oklahoma, Utah
and Wyoming, USA. Ate plants. 70 feet
(21m) long; weighed 33 tons. One of the
best-known dinosaurs. Has also been
called Brontosaurus ("thunder reptile).
Shorter than Diplodocus but much
heavier.

Lightly draw two overlapping
ovals for the body.

Make a much smaller, tilted
oval for the head. Notice how
far it is from the body.

From the top of the head,
draw a smooth curving line
touching the tops of larger
ovals to make the back.

Add the line for the bottom
of the neck. Add details to the
face.

Always start out **lightly!**

Using rods and joints (see pages 4-5), place the legs in the first two ovals you drew.

Then add thickness to the legs by making their outlines. Extend the belly line back to the beginning of the tail. Don't draw the bottom of the tail yet!

Add the curving line of the top of the tail.

Now add the bottom of the tail. Look at the way it runs into the other line. Draw the other line (shown with dashes) and you've got a tail that looks like it's curving.

Turn your drawing as you draw to avoid smudging it with your hand.

Triceratops

TRI-CER-A-TOPS

"Three-horned face"

Cretaceous; North America, from Alberta and Saskatchewan to Colorado and South Dakota. Up to 30 feet (9m) long; weighed 6 tons. Cores of the horns measure up to 3 ft (90cm); actual horns may have been much longer.

Draw a light, horizontal oval.

Using rods and joints (see pages 4-5), construct the front and rear leg. Make the hip higher than the shoulder.

Make the next joint higher in the rear leg than the front.

Notice how the legs bend toward each other.

Carefully outline the legs and draw the toes. Then lightly erase the rods and joints.

Now draw the other legs.

Always start out **lightly!**

Draw the tail, making the top and bottom of it blend right into the oval. Draw the shape of the head—very lightly!

Add the eye, nose, and mouth. Draw the three horns. Make the curved frill above the neck.

Finish your drawing by adding texture, shading, and background. (See pages 60-61 for ideas.)

Finally, clean up any smudges with your eraser.

T'riffic Triceratops!

While your pencil is sharp, go over fine details and make lines cleaner. When it starts to get dull, use it to add shading.

Parasaurolophus

PAR-A-SOR-O-LO-FUS

"Beside Sauralophus"

Cretaceous; Alberta, Utah and New Mexico. 33 feet long (10m). The long (up to 6 ft/1.8m) crest on its head was probably a visual signal to other dinosaurs. It might have supported brightly colored skin connected to the neck, like a flag or banner. It wasn't a snorkel!

Use the clock face to compare angles of lines and ovals.

Lightly draw an oval, with one end higher than the other.

Draw the closest two legs, using rods and joints (pages 4-5). Notice how much bigger the rear leg is than the front leg.

Add the other two legs, and the straight, pointed tail.

Lightly draw a circle for the head. Add the curving neck lines, then draw the crest on top. Add the snout.

Always start out lightly!

Now carefully erase lines where legs, neck, and tail overlap or join the body. Add eye and mouth. Begin shading in the darkest areas, on the far legs.

Wait a minute! What's going on here? It's turned around and stood up to take a better look at you!

It's easy to draw dinosaurs in different positions when you start with ovals. Try drawing this one on your own.

Remember to turn your drawing as you draw to avoid smudging it with your hand.

Ankylosaurus

AN-KY-LO-SAW-RUS

"Fused lizard"

Late Cretaceous; Alberta, Canada; Montana, USA. Up to 35 feet (10.7m) long. Built like an army tank. Swung its tail as a weapon, but with its armor plating, could have done well to simply hunker down when things started to get ugly. Some ankylosaurs had spikes along the sides; others didn't.

Draw a horizontal oval for the body. Add a pointed head on one end, and the tail on the other.

Use rods and joints (see pages 4-5) to draw the legs, then add their outlines. Notice the toenails!

Add the other two legs—notice where they join the body. Draw a line for the edge of the armor plating, all along the side. Draw eye and mouth, and horns on the face.

Carefully erase the rods and joints in the legs. Erase the main oval where the neck and tail join. Add a checkerboard pattern for the armor plates of the back, with a small bump in each square. Draw larger bumps on the neck and base of tail. Add a small row of bumps on the nose and tail.

Always start out lightly!

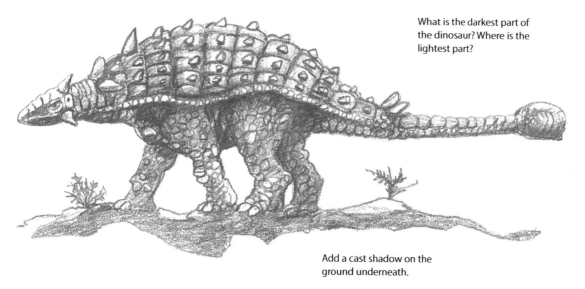

What is the darkest part of the dinosaur? Where is the lightest part?

Add a cast shadow on the ground underneath.

Finish your drawing by adding texture, shading, and background.

Turn your drawing as you draw to avoid smudging it with your hand.

Finally, clean up any smudges with your eraser.

Use your knowledge of ovals, rods and joints to make your ankylosaurus in different settings: perhaps using its tail as a weapon ...

Pachycephalosaurus

PAK-EE-SEF-O-LO-SAW-RUS

"Thick-headed lizard"

Cretaceous; western North America. 15 feet (4.6m) long. Scientists have decided that the extraordinarily thick (10 inch/25cm) skulls served as crash helmets, and that male dinosaurs would butt heads to establish dominance, as males of some species still do today.

Use the clock face to compare angles of lines and ovals.

Begin by drawing a slanted oval for the dinosaur's body.

Add two swooping lines for the tail. Draw a vertical oval for the head, and two lines for the neck.

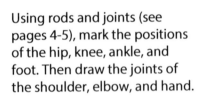

Using rods and joints (see pages 4-5), mark the positions of the hip, knee, ankle, and foot. Then draw the joints of the shoulder, elbow, and hand.

Add a line for the ground.

Outline the leg and arm.

Always start out lightly!

Add the other arm and leg. Carefully erase rods, joints, and parts of ovals that you don't want to show in the finished drawing. Draw the eye and mouth, and bony bumps atop the head.

Add shading and details.

Remember: while your pencil is sharp, go over fine details and make lines cleaner. As it gets duller, add shading.

Stegosaurus

STEG-O-SAW-RUS

"Roof lizard"

Biggest known stegosaurid. Late Jurassic; Colorado, Oklahoma, Utah and Wyoming, USA. Up to 30 feet (9m) long; weighed up to 2 tons. Spikes on end of tail for defense. Scientists debate what those big plates did, and whether they were staggered or in even pairs.

Use the clock face to compare angles of lines and ovals.

Draw a tilted, horizontal oval.

Draw a small, flat oval for the head, with a bump for the nose. Add two curving lines for the neck. Notice how the lines join the bottom of the big oval. They seem to flow right into it. Add lines for the tail, coming to a point at the end.

Using rods and joints (see pages 4-5), place the legs, then add outlines.

Add the remaining two legs. Draw the eye, nose and mouth. Carefully erase rods and joints, and parts of ovals that overlap. Darken the bottom outline.

Always start out **lightly!**

Draw a line of diamond-shaped armor plates along the back. Draw two tail spikes.

Add another row of plates. Make vertical lines on them. Draw the remaining two spikes on the tail.

Finish your drawing by adding texture and shading. Use your imagination! Did Stego have a camouflage pattern? Or perhaps stripes, like a zebra? And were those plates really bare, or perhaps supporting a fin on the back? Who knows?

Look at your drawing in a mirror (or through the back of the paper). It's amazing how different it looks. This gives you a good way to see parts that you can make better.

Kentrosaurus

KEN-TRO-SAW-RUS

"Pointed lizard"

Late Jurassic; Tanzania, East Africa. 17 feet (5m) long. Stegosaurus-like plates become spikes farther back. Extra spikes stuck out sideways from the hip.

Use the clock face to compare angles of lines and ovals.

Lightly draw a tilted oval.

Add two long, swooping lines for the tail, then draw a small oval for the head, and two lines for the neck. Draw the eye and mouth.

The bottom of the tail and the top of the neck are level.

Draw a line for the ground, and use rods and joints (see pages 4-5) to create the front leg.

Add the rear leg, using rods and joints (see pages 4-5).

Always start out **lightly**!

Now draw the other two legs. Look how one rear leg ends above the ground line. When you add the shadow underneath, it will appear that you're looking slightly down at the dinosaur.

Add pairs of pointed plates on the front half of the dinosaur, and pairs of spikes on the back. Notice the extra pair of spikes on the hip. Turn your paper sideways to make it easier to draw the spikes.

Extra spikes on the hips

Now, carefully erase overlapping ovals, rods, and joints. Add the cast shadow.

cast shadow

Add shading and shadows. Notice the shadows on the dinosaur's back from its plates and spikes.

Finally, clean up any smudges with your eraser.

Kool kentrosaur!

Maiasaura

MY-A-SOR-A

"Good mother lizard"

Cretaceous; Montana, USA. Up to 30 feet (9m) long. In 1978 scientists discovered fossilized baby Maiasaura and eggs around a mound-shaped nest, the first evidence of dinosaurs with organized family structure.

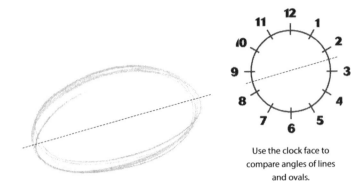

Use the clock face to compare angles of lines and ovals.

Start with a tilted oval for the dinosaur's body.

Notice the angle of the eye

Look where the top of the tail joins the body. From that point, draw the line for the top of the tail. Then add the bottom of the tail, which flows smoothly into the bottom of the oval.

Draw a circle for the head. Place the eye inside it. Add the curving lines of the neck, flowing into the ovals at either end.

Using rods and joints (see pages 4-5), draw the hip, knee, ankle, and foot. Lightly add the outline of the leg.

Repeat for the arm. Make the hand higher than the foot. Draw lines for the inside and outside of the nest. Draw eggs in the nest.

outside of nest

inside of nest

! You only see part of each egg.

Always start out **lightly!**

Now add the other leg and arm. Draw the mouth and nostril.

Carefully erase rods and joints, and overlapping sections of the main oval. Then go over the outlines and begin to add details.

Finish your drawing by adding texture, shading, shadows, and background.

Clean up any smudges with your eraser.

Mahvelous Maiasaura!

Plesiosaurus

PLEES-EE-O-SAW-RUS

"Ribbon reptile."

Jurassic; Germany, England. 6-28 feet long (2-9m). Swam by flapping front flippers up and down. Probably moved its neck very quickly to catch fish. Alas, not a dinosaur but a swimming reptile.

Draw a horizontal oval for the body, and a smaller one for the head.

Draw the swooping lines of the neck. Add the tail. Draw the centerline of the back.

Add limbs, with flippers instead of feet.

Draw the mouth and eye. Carefully erase the original oval at neck and tail.

Add shading to add form to the body, and you have a …

… pleasing Plesiosaurus!

Trianglesaurs

When you look at your subject, you may spot curving lines that are easy to draw. Or it might seem obvious to start with an oval.

But sometimes, triangles will jump out at you. When looking at reference material such as pictures in books, use the approach that makes the most sense to you.

Can you spot the dinosaurs lurking in these triangles?

Looking for Triangles

When artists and illustrators sit down to draw a realistic picture, they almost always have some sort of reference material. In other words, they look at something as they draw it.

But no people see things exactly alike.

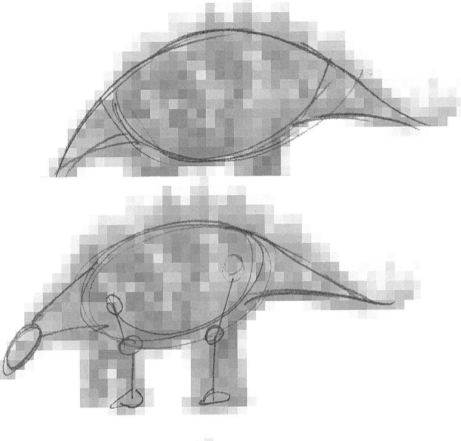

One person might see big swooping lines and start the drawing as a linosaur.

Another person might start with an oval for the body, making an ovalsaur.

And a third person might see triangles, and use them to begin the drawing.

Triangles are everywhere. When you look at your subject, look for curving lines and look for ovals. Also look for triangles.

Always start out **lightly**!

A right triangle has one angle that is square

There are no rules to this type of drawing. Just keep looking until you find something—whether a line, an oval, or a triangle—that helps you get your drawing started. As with the other drawing techniques, you need to start out very lightly! Let's do a quick sketch to see how it works.

Draw a right triangle.

Add another right triangle for the tail. Draw a curve to round out the back. Add a round shape for the head.

Add the most obvious triangles of all – the plates on its back.

Draw triangles for feet, making them look very firmly planted on the ground. Use open triangles to connect with the knees, and you have the beginning of some solid-looking legs!

Add details, shading, and shadows as before.

Tyrannosaurus

TIE-RAN-O-SAW-RUS

"Tyrant lizard"

Cretaceous; western North America, China.
Ate meat. Lots of it. 39 feet (12m) long;
18.5 feet (5.6m) tall; weighed 7 tons—
as much as an African elephant. Skull
measured 4 feet (1.2m). Saw-edged teeth
could be 7 inches (18cm) long.

Start by drawing (very lightly!)
a right triangle.

Draw another long triangle
connecting to it and pointing
downward.

Using more triangles, make
the shape of the thigh and
calf of the dinosaur. Add part
of a triangle for the other leg.
Notice how the triangles look
like legs already!

Make single lines for the
bottom part of the leg, and
small triangles for the feet.
Draw one foot at an angle
and slightly higher. What is it
touching?

A right triangle has
one angle that is
square

42   *Draw Dinosaurs*

Always start out **lightly!**

Add two triangles for the head. You now have a pattern of triangles that looks like Tyrannosaurus!

Looking at the finished example, round the triangles by making outlines of the tail, back, belly, legs, and head.

Add the arms.

If you drew your triangles very lightly, you can carefully use your eraser and make them disappear before finishing your drawing. If not, you may want to start over–making the triangles very light this time!

Add details to your finished drawing. Use your imagination!

Remember: use your pencil for different things as it goes from sharp to dull.

Velociraptor

VEL-OS-I-RAP-TOR

"Swift plunderer"

Late Cretaceous; Mongolia, China, and Khazakhstan. 6 feet (1.8m) long. Probably hunted in packs, attacking with claws and teeth. In 1971 a specimen was found that had died while attacking a Protoceratops.

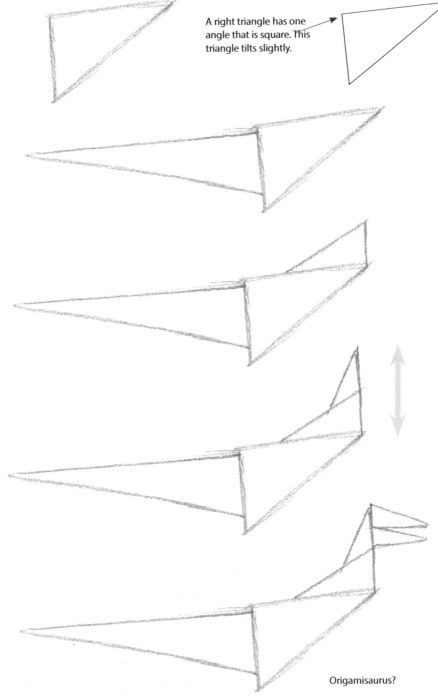

Start your raptor drawing with a slightly tilted right triangle.

A right triangle has one angle that is square. This triangle tilts slightly.

Add a second, much longer triangle for the tail.

Draw a third triangle above the first triangle …

… and yet another triangle above it, the triangles' edges creating a vertical line.

Now make two triangles for the jaws.

Origamisaurus?

Draw a big and a small triangle for the leg. Add a line for the lower leg, and toes.

Erase lines that you no longer need.

Add two arms, and the other leg, using rods and joints (see pages 4-5). Enhance the outline of the dinosaur by making the belly, neck, and jaws bigger.

Finish your drawing by adding texture, shading, and background. (See pages 60-61 for ideas.)

Remember to turn your drawing as you draw to avoid smudging it with your hand. Clean up any smudges with your eraser.

Compsognathus

KOMP-sog-NATH-us

"Pretty jaw"

Jurassic; southern Germany, southeast France. Ate small animals. Up to 2 feet (60cm) long. This chicken-sized dinosaur probably lived and hunted in small herds, possibly attacking larger animals in a group.

A right triangle has one angle that is square. This triangle tilts slightly.

Start by lightly drawing a right triangle.

Add another right triangle pointing the other direction. Make the tops of both form a straight line.

From the end of the first triangle, make another triangle sticking up for the neck …

… and from it, a triangle sticking out for the head.

Lightly draw a titling triangle to make the top of the leg.

Erase parts of triangles when you no longer need them, or if they become confusing.

Use the clock face to compare angles.

Always start out **lightly!**

Complete the leg with rods and joints (see pages 4-5). Add rods and joints for the other leg and arm.

Now add the round curves of the outline, following the example.

Finish your drawing by adding texture, shading, and background.

- Look at your drawing in a mirror (or through the back of the paper) to spot areas you can improve.

- While your pencil is sharp, go over fine details and make lines cleaner. As it gets duller, add shading.

- Turn your drawing as you draw to avoid smudging it with your hand.

- Finally, clean up any smudges with your eraser.

Deinonychus

die-no-NIKE-us

"Terrible claw"

Early Cretaceous; Montana, USA. 10-13 feet (3-4m) long. Larger then Velociraptor, it could kick into the belly of an animal and tear it open with its large (5 inch/12.7cm) scythe-like claw. There were also three heavy claws on each hand, with powerful arm muscles to make them effective weapons. This would be a dinosaur to avoid!

Always start out lightly!

A right triangle has one angle that is square

Start by lightly drawing a right triangle for the body.

Add another triangle pointing up, the other direction, for the tail.

Make another triangle on top of the first …

… and from it, two triangles for the jaws. Draw the eye.

Add two more triangles to make the top and bottom parts of the leg.

Using rods and joints (see pages 4-5), draw the foot with its sickle claw, and add the other leg and foot. Draw the arms.

Now add the round curves of the outline, following the example. Erase lines you no longer need.

Finish your drawing by adding texture, shading, and background.

Clean up any smudges with your eraser.

Dynamite Deinonychus!

Pteranodon

TER-AN-O-DON

"Winged toothless"

Late Cretaceous; Wyoming, USA. Wing span of 23 feet (7m); greater than any known bird. Probably only weighed about 37 lbs (17kg). Long, toothless jaw was counterbalanced by bony crest at top of head. Probably scooped fish out of the ocean, as pelicans do today – and probably had a pelican-like pouch as well.

There's no right or wrong way to use triangles in drawing. Just remember that they can be a handy tool.

For example, you may not need all the triangles I used in the Pteranodon's wing. Use as many as you find helpful!

When you finish a drawing, put the date on it, and keep it with your others. You might be surprised to see how much better you've become with practice!

Solidsaurs

As your dinosaur drawings improve, you may want the extra challenge of making dinosaurs that look as though they're coming right toward you.

In order to do this, it helps to understand basic forms and how to draw them.

Basic forms

To draw solidsaurs, you'll find three forms most useful: cylinders, cones, and rounded forms based on ovals.

Shading makes your solid form look solid.

But for shading to work, it needs to follow the contours of the form. The middle drawing of each form shows contour lines. When you add shading, make the lines of the shading follow these lines.

Combined, the forms can make bodies, legs, and more with greater realism.

Cylinder

Cone

Rounded form

Using solid forms, you can choose whether to do serious, realistic drawings or make funny drawings and cartoon characters. In any case, understanding forms and contour lines will help make your drawings look more three-dimensional.

These heads were drawn using a box, another common form.

Lambeosaurus

LAM-be-oh-SAW-rus

"Lambe's lizard"

Cretaceous; western North America. About 50 feet (15m) long. The tall, showy head crest was a hollow bone. The nostrils ran up from the snout through the crest.

Start with a vertical, slightly tilted oval for the body. Add the lines for the tail. Draw the oval for the head, with eye and crest. Add almost vertical neck lines. Draw the centerline of the body.

Use a combination of cylinders and cones to draw the leg, with curving lines showing the contours. Add more contour lines on the tail and belly.

Add the other leg and arms.

Always start out **lightly!**

Finish details in the head and neck, and add more shading to round out the body.

Finish your drawing by adding texture, shading, and background. Finally, clean up any smudges with your eraser.

Lovely Lambeosaurus!

Remember these drawing tips:

Look at your drawing in a mirror (or through the back of the paper) to spot areas you can improve.

While your pencil is sharp, go over fine details and make lines cleaner. As it gets duller, add shading.

Turn your drawing as you draw to avoid smudging it with your hand.

Scelidosaurus

SKEL-**IDE**-OH-**SOR**-US

"Limb lizard"

Early Jurassic; southern England, Tibet. 13 feet (4 m) long. Probably a slow-moving dinosaur, it had very sturdy legs and was armored with bony knobs on its back. It's one of the few dinosaurs where fossils show an impression of the skin!

Use the clock face to compare angles of lines and ovals.

Draw a flat, tilted oval with contour lines showing the form.

Add the neck and head. Use contour lines wrapping around the neck to create foreshortening (making it look like it's coming toward you). Add other lines where the rows of bumps will be on the back.

Using cylinders, draw the front leg.

Always start out **lightly**!

With more cylinders, draw the rear leg and the foot, and the only visible portion of the other front leg.

Draw the tail. Lightly erase lines you no longer need, then add the rows of bumps on the back.

Finish your drawing by adding texture, shading, shadows, and background.

Segnosaurus

SEG-no-SAW-rus

"Slow lizard"

Cretaceous; southeast Mongolia. May have been 30 feet (9m) long. This dinosaur is known only from a partial skeleton. The best guess is that it might have been a swimmer and fed on fish.

Use the clock face to compare angles of lines and ovals.

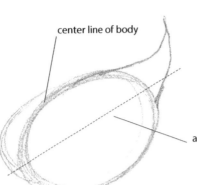

center line of body

axis of tilted oval

Draw a tilted oval. Add the center line of the body, and extend it to make the top of the tail. Add the bottom line of the tail.

With cylinders, rods and joints, draw the back leg. Make contour lines wrapping around the leg and the body.

Add the arm. Shade the area behind it to make a dark shadow. The contrast of the dark makes the light arm appear closer.

Add the other arm and leg in a similar manner.

Always start out **lightly**!

Draw the neck and head. Use contour lines to show the form of the neck.

Finish your drawing by adding texture, shading, and background. Clean up any smudges with your eraser.

Sensational Segnosaurus!

Turn your drawing as you draw to avoid smudging it with your hand.

Finishing Touches

Before you add shading or texture, carefully remove lines that you don't want in the finished drawing.

It's OK if you erase some of the "good" lines. You'll go over them again to "sharpen" them.

Erase lines you don't need in the final drawing: rods and joints, and where parts overlap.

A kneadable eraser starts out square, but you bend and twist it so you can erase small areas. If you can find one, you'll use it often.

Some paper erases well. Some paper doesn't. Don't be discouraged if erasing messes up your drawing, but do try to find a good "erasing" paper. Draw more lightly next time so you don't have as much to erase!

Next, build tones (light and dark) by shading with a dull pencil. Don't just scribble with your pencil in every direction: follow the contours of the form.

With a blending stump or small rolled-up wad of paper, you can smudge the shading to make it very smooth.

While your pencil is sharp, add details and texture. Go over lines, making them sharper and stronger.

Add patterns to the skin, making them follow the contours of the body whenever possible.

A blending stump looks like a pencil made of paper. Use it or a rolled-up wad of paper to smooth shaded areas

Follow contours when you shade. In the lower box, the stripes and shading show a curved contour, similar to the curve of an arm for leg. In contrast, the upper box looks flat.

Backgrounds

Adding background details can make your drawing much more fun to look at. For a quick background, draw a squiggly line of mountains. Add another, and another. Notice how the hills in front overlap those further away.

Add plants, simple or complicated:

A

B

C

A. Simple pencil strokes suggest grass, and create a sense of scale for this small dinosaur.

B. Bushier plants make this dino look larger.

C. Smaller plants farther away help create a sense of depth.

D

 E

D. Broad, leafy plants as tall as the dinosaur add realism to the drawing.

E. Plants that hardly reach its knees make the dinosaur look bigger. But the volcano looks bigger still! Notice overlapping.

Use your imagination!

Have fun!

Some final thoughts

Remember…

One of the great secrets of our world is that behind every success there's always plenty of practice. The people who do amazing feats of daring, skill, or ingenuity have been practicing, often for much longer than you'd imagine. They've probably failed more often than you can imagine, too, so don't waste time being discouraged. If your drawings don't look exactly the way you'd like them to (especially the first try), stop, look, and try again!

Save your drawings!

Whenever you do a drawing—or even a sketch—put your initials (or autograph!) and date on it. And save it. You don't have to save it until it turns yellow and crumbles to dust, but do keep your drawings, at least for several months. Sometimes, hiding in your portfolio, they will mysteriously improve! I've seen it happen often with my own drawings, especially the ones I knew were no good at all, but kept anyway.

If you don't have your own portfolio, here's a way to make one inexpensively (or you can buy one at an art supply store).

Tape (both sides)

String (to tie portfolio closed)

Cardboard   Cardboard

Do-it-yourself portfolio

Index

Have you enjoyed this book? We'd
love a review online!

When they lived
(images not to scale)

Cretaceous period—55 to 65 million years ago

Jurassic period—66 to 145 million years ago

Made in the USA
San Bernardino,
CA

58734366R00038